Too Much Talk!

Retold by Sean Taylor

Illustrated by Ofra Amit

One day a farmer was digging his field.
He started pulling a yam out of the soil
and a voice said,
"You did not weed me! You did not
water me! And now you are going to
pull me up!"

The farmer was amazed.

"Who said that?" he asked.

"Not me," said his dog.

The farmer was so amazed
that he ran away down the hill.

A fisherman looked round at him.
"A yam talked to me!" shouted the farmer.
"Then a dog talked to me!"

"How can that be true? That is not possible," said the fisherman.

"Yes it is," said a fish in his basket.

The fisherman was so amazed
that he ran after the farmer.

A woman was swimming down the river.
She looked round at the men.
"A yam, a dog and a fish talked to us!"
shouted the farmer and the fisherman.

"How can that be true? That is not possible," said the woman.
"Yes it is," said the river.

The woman was so amazed
that she ran after them too.

They went to tell the Chief.

"A yam, a dog, a fish and a river talked to us!" said the farmer and the fisherman and the woman.

The Chief got up from his chair.
"That is not possible," he said.
"Yams can't talk. Dogs can't talk.
Fish can't talk. And rivers can't talk.
Now stop wasting my time before
I throw you all in jail!"

The farmer, the fisherman and the
woman left in a hurry.
"A talking yam!" said the Chief.
"What nonsense!"
"Quite right," said his chair.